Isabelle Leloup

Cross-stitch and Embroidery
for Babies, Toddlers and Children

Photography by Hiroko Mori
Styling by Vania Leroy-Thuillier

Project charts by Isabelle Faidy-Contreau

M U R D O C H   B O O K S

This book is dedicated to sweet Nathalie,
creator of Lili Points...

Contents

Just so we're clear, I don't know how to embroider.

I can sense your disappointment. It all began a very long time ago (I am very, very old). The revolution of May '68 had come and gone, the now-renowned craft store La Droguerie had just opened in Paris, the craft magazine *100 Idées* was wreaking havoc on the news stands and my siblings and I were the kings of DIY.

Almost always in fancy dress, we grew up in the shadow of a band of cheerful lunatics hooked on pottery, drawing, weaving, and tapestry. In fact, I think my parents grew up with us. I learned with them that there's no point being afraid of failing; at worst, you have to start again and that's not a drama …

I started by watching maman, a true handicrafts activist! We achieved works of art together … from the painted walls of our country bedroom to surrealist fringes cut with nail-scissors – what a bad quarter of an hour that was – painting, clay, plaster, enamels, stained glass windows and silk painting … We covered everything, and the dirtier we ended up, the happier she was!

I watched her sew, paint, knit and embroider on everything that crossed her path. The clothes she made for us, the pieces of fabric she put together; even a friend's wedding dress went under the needle. I remember her dress with motifs in every colour, like something from Peru, or the jeans with embroidered flowers on my bottom that I was ashamed of at school.

She began using a line drawing that she then filled in with coloured threads, both matte and shiny. I did the same. I must have been 7 or 8 years old. And then I kept going, serving with my grandmother, cooking alongside my father … knitting and crochet were the only things that never stuck (not that my other grandmother didn't try her best!). Apart from that, I can rampage through pretty much everything!

When little ones began to spring up around me, I designed clothes for them and then I embroidered them; it was the obvious thing to do – and it was less expensive. Then the magazines *Marie-Claire Idées* and *De Fil en Aiguille* came along …

Today, I am a painter, as one of my sisters is as well, maman 'watercolours' and makes bits and pieces with her grandchildren, papa no longer does tapestry but frames everyone's drawings. The fact that all of these family adventures are at the heart of this book makes me laugh a lot and also makes me very nostalgic for this mad childhood – but proud of it as well.

So, please, by all means change the colours, mix up the designs, take away a few stitches and add a few as well and use any canvas you please. Above all, create and enjoy: it's the only thing that counts.

n° 1

cot canopy
instructions page *57* • chart page *95*

n° 2

jewellery bib
instructions page **58** • chart page **94**

n° 3
love bib
instructions page **59** • chart page **95**

n° 4
dressing box
instructions page *60* • charts pages *96-97*

樱 桃
yīng táo
cherry
さくらんぼ

n°ˢ 5 & 6

strawberry and heart t-shirts
instructions page *61* • charts page *130*

n° 7

angel sleeping bag
instructions page *61* • chart pages *98-99*

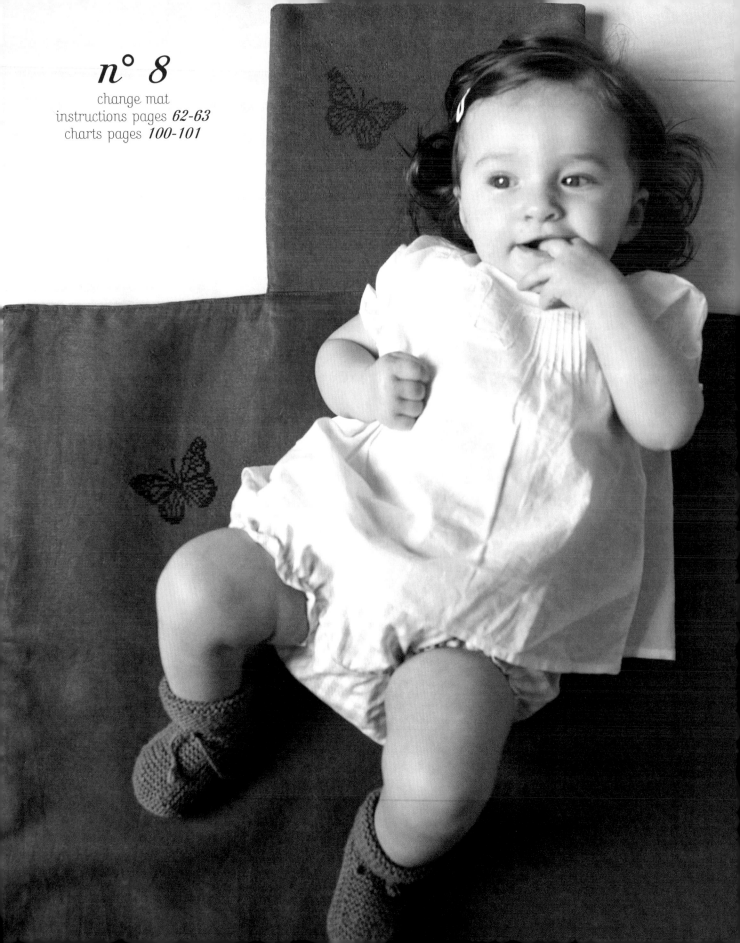

n° 8
change mat
instructions pages *62-63*
charts pages *100-101*

n° 9
bird-on-a-wire cushion
instructions page *64* • chart pages *102-103*

n° 10

A to Z alphabet
instructions page **65** • chart pages *104-107*

n° 11
little letters
instructions page **65** • charts pages *104-107*

n° 12

chinese suit
instructions page *66* • chart pages *108-109*

n° 13
good luck bib
instructions page **67** • chart page **111**

n° 14

carry-all

instructions pages *68-69* • chart pages *112-113*

n^{os} *15 & 16*

stars and moon t-shirts
instructions page *70* • charts page *131*

n° 17
fit-for-a-queen bib
instructions page *70* • chart page *114*

n⁰ˢ *18 & 19*

sheet and pillowcase
instructions page *71* • charts page *115*

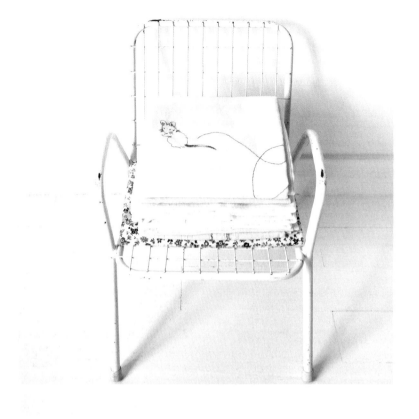

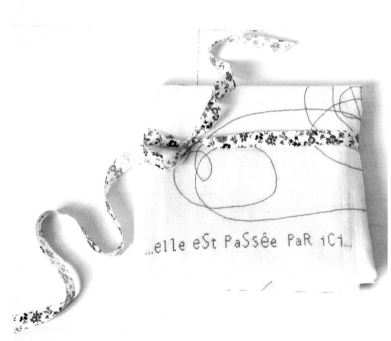

...elle eSt PaSSée PaR iCi...

n° 20
this-way-and-that-way quilt cover
instructions page *72* • chart and pattern pages *116-117*

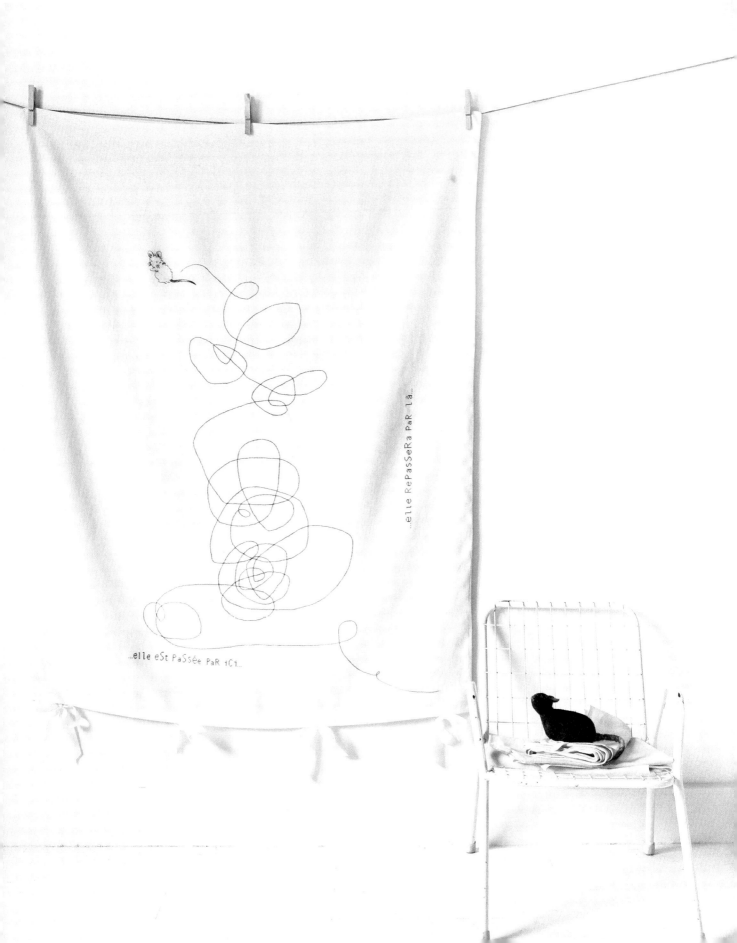

...elle RePaSSeRa PaR là...

...elle eSt PaSSée PaR iCi...

n° 22
little horror bib
instructions page *74* • chart page *119*

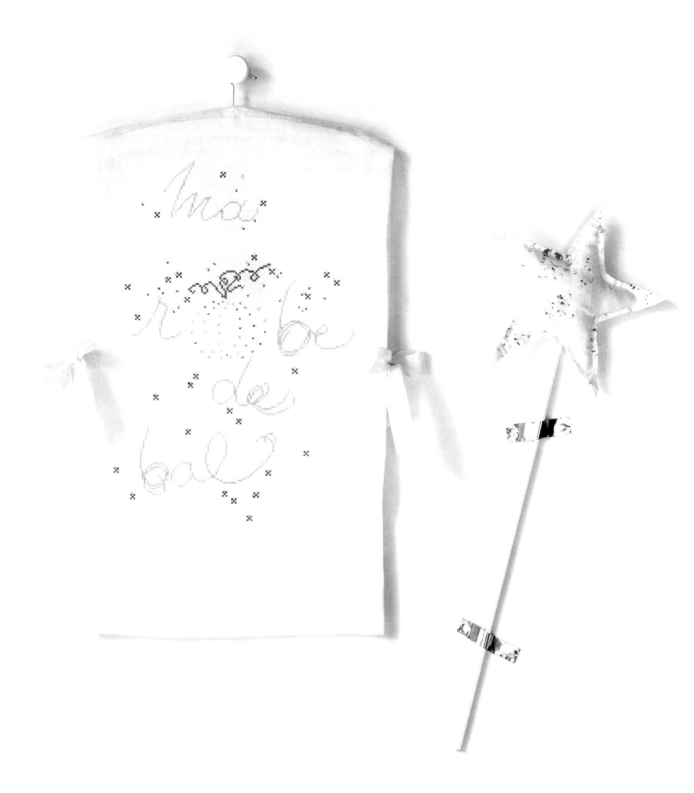

n° 23

my-ball-gown dress cover
instructions page *75* • chart pages *120–121*

n° 24
counting geese dress
instructions page *76* • charts page *122*

n° 25
a-star-is-born cushion
instructions page *77* • chart page *123*

n° 25 (variation)
moon cushion
instructions page 77 • chart page 123

n° 26

quilt
instructions page *78* • chart page *126*

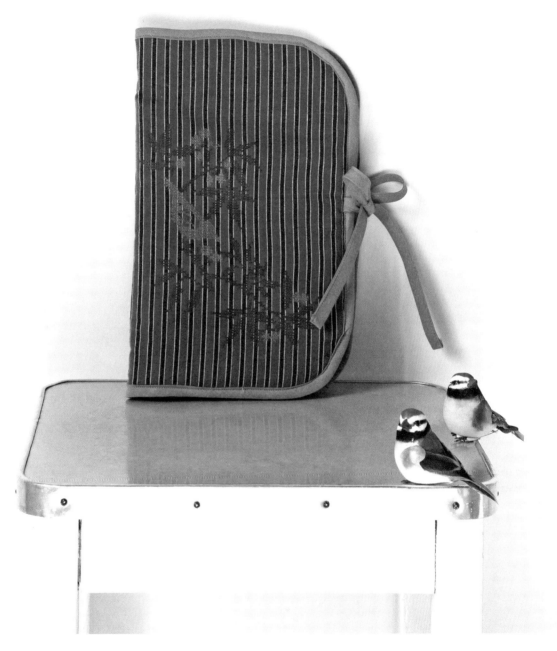

n° 28
health record booklet cover
instructions page *80* • chart page *127*

n° 29
bathrobe
instructions page *81* • chart page *140*

n° 30
t-shirt
instructions page *81* • chart page *130*

n° 31
Lucie embroidery
instructions page *82* • charts pages *128–129 and 134*

n° 31 (variation)

Lucie cushion

instructions page *82* • charts pages *128–129 and 134*

n° 32

bouquet embroidery
instructions page *82* • chart pages *136–139*

n° 33
little girl purse
instructions page *83* • chart pages *132–133*

LA CHICORÉE

n° 34
little guy embroidery
instructions page *84* • chart pages *132–133*

n° 35
counting sheep curtain
instructions page *85* • charts and pattern page *135*

n° 36
butterfly jumpsuit
instructions page *86* • chart page *95*

n° 37
just-a-minute bottle cover
instructions page *87* • chart page *140*

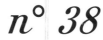

n° 38

cot bumper
instructions page *88* • chart page *141*

n° 39

alphabet sampler
instructions page *89* • chart pages *142–143*

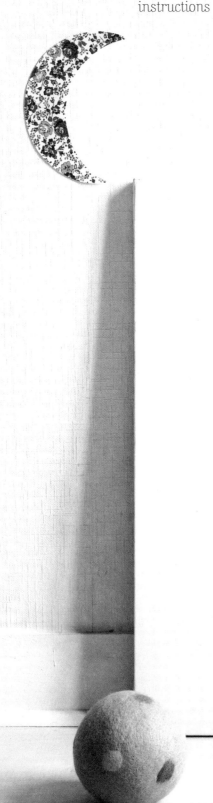

Please note: Many of the projects in this book are worked on 40-count linen, which has 16 threads (or 8 stitches) per centimetre and is very fine. If you would prefer to work on a larger linen, then by all means do so, but remember that the finished design will be larger, so be sure to work out whether it will fit on the project you have chosen by counting the number of stitches on the chart.

n° 1

cot canopy
photo page 6 • chart page 95
4 m soft pink tulle • size 28 tapestry needle
1 skein DMC Mouliné stranded cotton: 963
stitch used: cross-stitch

The advantage of tulle is that there is no need to hem it; you just need to make sure you cut it straight. The structure of the fabric also makes it easy to cross-stitch.

Cross-stitch over 1 thread of tulle with 1 strand of Mouliné cotton. Follow your imagination and put the butterflies wherever it takes your fancy, but try to put them mostly close to the edge, otherwise they will become lost in the folds and gathers of the canopy.

1. 10 m

4 m

n° 2

jewellery bib
photo page 7 • chart page 94
30 x 45 cm 40-count linen • 30 x 45 cm waffle-weave fabric
30 x 45 cm cotton print • 2.5 m bias binding • size 28 tapestry needle
1 skein DMC Mouliné stranded cotton: 603, 815 and S602
stitch used: cross-stitch

Cut the three fabric rectangles into a bib shape, following the pattern on pages 90–91, then cross-stitch the motif over 2 threads in the centre of the piece of linen, using 1 strand of Mouliné cotton. Lay the cotton print fabric out flat, wrong side up, and place the waffle-weave fabric and linen on top, right side up. Pin the bias binding around the outside of the bib, then around the neck opening, as per the diagram below, and stitch, first around the outside of the bib and then around the neck opening.

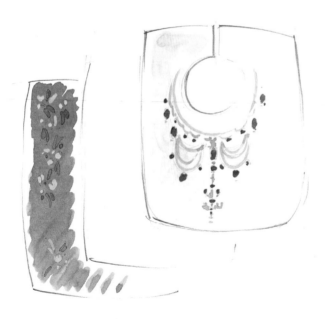

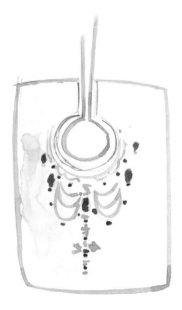

n° 3

love bib

photo page 8 • chart page 95
29 x 31 cm 40-count linen • 29 x 31 cm waffle-weave fabric
29 x 31 cm cotton print • 29 x 10 cm cotton with a contrast print • 1.8 m bias binding
1 skein DMC Mouliné stranded cotton: S712 and 415 • size 28 tapestry needle
stitch used: cross-stitch

Cut the three large rectangles of fabric into a bib shape, following the pattern on page 110. Trim the bottom of the contrast cotton print to make rounded corners, like the bottom of the bib, then cross-stitch the motif on the linen over 2 threads, using 1 strand of Mouliné cotton.

Place the fabric for the false pocket on the linen, right sides together, as per the diagram, stitch across the straight edge, and fold the cotton print back on top of the bottom of the piece of linen. Lay the cotton print out flat, wrong side up, and place the waffle-weave fabric and the linen on top, right side up. Pin the bias binding around the outside of the bib, then around the neck opening, as per the diagram, and stitch – first around the outside of the bib and then around the neck opening.

n° 4

dressing box
photo page 9 • charts pages 96–97
1 shallow wooden or firm cardboard box, preferably with sloping sides
white 40-count linen • cotton print for the lining • 2.4 m organza ribbon
1 skein DMC Mouliné stranded cotton: E168 • size 28 tapestry needle
stitch used: cross-stitch

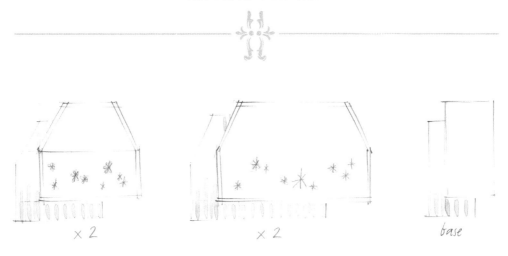

× 2   × 2   base

Adjusting the designs above to the size of your box, and remembering to add 1-cm seam allowance, cut each side pattern twice (base x 1) from both linen and cotton. Cut the ribbon into eight equal pieces.

Cross-stitch the motifs on the sides of the linen pieces, using 1 strand of Mouliné cotton over 2 threads of linen. Next, sew the four sides and the linen base together as per the diagram opposite, then press open the seams. Do the same with the cotton lining. Place the two assembled pieces on top of each other, right sides together, and insert the pieces of ribbon between the two layers, as per the diagram. Stitch all around, 1 cm from the edge, so that one end of each piece of ribbon is secured in the seam, leaving one side open. Turn right side out, turn in 1cm on the raw edge of each side of the opening, iron the assembled piece and sew the opening closed by hand. Place the box inside the cover and tie the ribbons together.

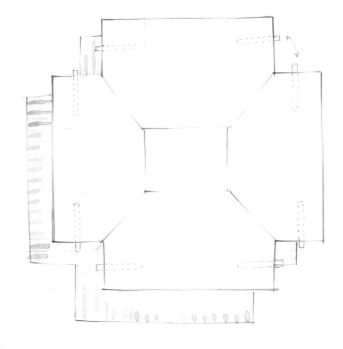

n°s 5 & 6

strawberry and heart t-shirts

photos pages 10–11 • charts page 130

1 coloured t-shirt • DMC 14-count soluble waste canvas • size 26 tapestry needle

1 skein DMC Mouliné stranded cotton: 471, 947 and 150 for the strawberry t-shirt

1 skein DMC Mouliné stranded cotton: S602 for the heart t-shirt

stitches used: cross-stitch and straight stitch

Attach a piece of soluble canvas using large basting stitches to the place you will be embroidering. Begin the embroidery in the centre of the canvas and cross-stitch over 1 thread with 2 strands of Mouliné cotton, working through both layers. Remove the soluble canvas by placing the t-shirt under water and and rubbing carefully.

n° 7

angel sleeping bag

photos pages 12–13 • chart pages 98–99

1 sleeping bag • DMC 14-count soluble waste canvas

1 skein DMC Mouliné stranded cotton: 451 • size 26 tapestry needle

stitch used: cross-stitch

Attach two pieces of soluble canvas to the top of the back of the sleeping bag using large basting stitches. Begin embroidering the motif in the centre of the soluble canvas and cross-stitch over 1 thread of canvas with 2 strands of Mouliné cotton. Remove the soluble canvas by placing the sleeping bag under water and rubbing carefully.

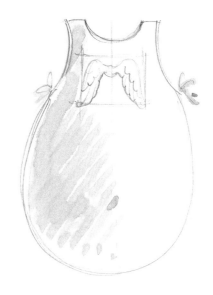

n° 8

change mat

photo page 14 • charts pages 100–101
2 pieces 40-count linen, each 64 x 89 cm, for the mattress
26 x 46 cm 40-count linen, for the pillow
62 x 87 cm batting for the mattress • 24 x 21 cm batting for the pillow
DMC 14-count soluble waste canvas • 1 large button • 10 cm bias binding
1 skein DMC Mouliné stranded cotton: 777, 600, 150 and 154 • size 26 tapestry needle
stitch used: cross-stitch

Cut two pieces of soluble canvas and attach one to each large linen rectangle using large basting stitches. (Since the mat will be folded for carrying, make sure you won't be embroidering on a fold line.)

Following the guidelines of the diagrams below and opposite, cross-stitch the butterflies over 1 threads of canvas using 2 strands of Mouliné cotton, beginning the motif in the centre of the soluble canvas and working through both layers. Remove the pieces of soluble canvas by placing the fabric under water and rubbing carefully.

Place the two rectangles of linen together, right sides facing each other. Fold the bias binding in half lengthways and stitch the edges together. Fold it in half into a loop and insert it between the two layers of fabric, in the middle of one of the long sides, raw edges matching. Stitch all around, 1 cm from the edge, leaving the upper shorter edge open. Turn right side out and press, pressing under 1cm on the raw edge of each side of the opening. Slip the batting inside.

For the pillow, embroider a butterfly on one half of the linen rectangle (using waste canvas as for the mattress), then fold the fabric right sides together and stitch the sides, 1 cm from the edge. Turn right side out, press and insert the batting inside. Slip the raw edges of the pillow between the upper edges of the mattress, keeping the pillow centred, then topstitch through all layers. Sew on the button to the long side of the mattress to correspond with the loop.

n° 9

bird-on-a-wire cushion
photo page 15 • chart pages 102–103
2 pieces 40-count linen, each 42 x 41 cm • size 28 tapestry needle
1 skein DMC Mouliné stranded cotton: 154 and 3041
stitch used: cross-stitch

Cross-stitch the motif over 2 threads of linen with 1 strand of Mouliné cotton on the top left of one piece of fabric, with the raw edge at the botton. Next, place the two linen rectangles right sides together, and turn up a 10 cm flap at the front and back. Iron to press the fold of the flaps and stitch the sides and top of the cushion, 1 cm from the edge. Turn right side out and press.

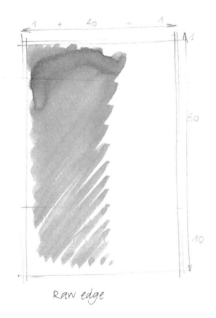

Raw edge

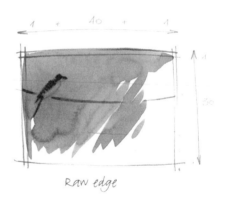

Raw edge

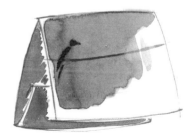

n° 10

A to Z alphabet

photos pages 16–17 • chart pages 104–107

30 x 150 cm white 40-count linen • size 28 tapestry needle

1 skein DMC Mouliné stranded cotton: 3348, 3364, 3363, 522, 3052 and 3051

stitch used: cross-stitch

Begin the motif in the centre of the fabric, starting with the letter M, cross-stitching over 2 threads of linen with 1 strand of Mouliné cotton. Leave a space of about 4 cm between each letter and make sure you leave a margin of at least 5 cm all around your embroidery.

n° 11

little letters

photo page 18 • chart pages 104–109

15 x 15 cm white 40-count linen • size 28 tapestry needle

1 skein DMC Mouliné stranded cotton: 3348, 3364, 3363, 522, 3052 and 3051

stitch used: cross-stitch

Begin the letter you have chosen in the middle of the piece of fabric. Cross-stitch over 2 threads of linen using 1 strand of Mouliné cotton, and make sure you leave a margin of at least 5 cm round your embroidery.

n° 12

chinese suit

photos pages 20–21 • chart pages 108–109

1 blue chinese suit

DMC 14-count soluble waste canvas • size 26 tapestry needle

1 skein DMC Mouliné stranded cotton: E168, 3844, 3760, 471, 154, 3809, 500, 522 and 947

stitches used: cross stitch, straight stitch and backstitch

Wash the suit to remove excess dye, otherwise the colour will run into your embroidery in the first wash. Unpick the pockets to be embroidered, and attach a piece of soluble canvas to the front of them sing large basting stitches.

Following the guidelines of the diagrams below, cross-stitch the motifs over 1 thread with 2 strands of Mouliné cotton, beginning in the centre of the soluble canvas. Embroider the other motifs in the same way, except the squiggly lines between the motifs, which don't require soluble canvas. Remove the pieces of soluble canvas by placing the pieces in water and rubbing carefully. Next, sew the pockets back on by machine, then work the squiggly lines of embroidery.

n° 13

good luck bib
photo page 22 • chart page 111
29 x 31 cm 40-count linen • 29 x 31 cm waffle-weave fabric
29 x 31 cm cotton print • 1.8 m bias binding • size 28 tapestry needle
1 skein DMC Mouliné stranded cotton: 154, S471 and S 472
stitches used: cross-stitch and straight stitch

Cut out the three rectangles of fabric following the pattern on page 110, then cross-stitch the motif over 2 threads with 1 strand of Mouliné cotton in the centre of the piece of linen. Lay the cotton print out flat, wrong side up, and place the waffle-weave fabric and linen on top, right side up.

Pin the bias binding around the outside of the bib, then around the neck opening, as per the diagram, and stitch, first around the outside of the bib and then the neck opening.

n° 14

carry-all

photo page 23 • chart pages 112–113

35 x 80 cm moss-green 36-count linen

35 x 68 cm cotton print for the lining

2 x 2.5-m lengths moss-green grosgrain ribbon • size 28 tapestry needle

1 skein DMC Mouliné stranded cotton: 3819, 471 and 469

stitch used: cross-stitch

Cross-stitch the motif over 1 thread of linen with 1 strand of Mouliné cotton in the centre of one half of the piece of linen. Fold the linen in half, right sides together, insert the two pieces of ribbon between the two layers as per the diagram opposite, so that one end of each piece is sewn into the bottom of the side seams.

Stitch the sides, leaving a 1.5 cm opening 5 cm from the top of each side. Turn over the top edge towards the wrong side, first 1 cm, then 3 cm, and press.

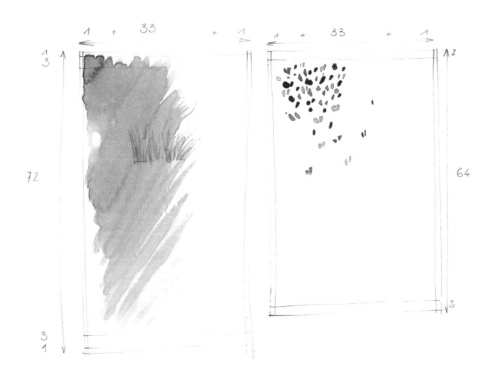

Fold the cotton in half, right sides together, and stitch the sides. Turn right side out, turn under 1 cm around the top edge and press. Slip the linen bag inside its cotton lining, wrong sides facing, and slip the folded edge of the lining 5 mm under the edge of the linen hem.

Stitch all around, a few millimetres from the edge of the cotton lining, then turn the bag right side out. Thread one ribbon through the drawstring casing, around the bag then out again on the same side and sew the end back onto the ribbon at the bottom of the bag, as per the diagram. Do the same with the other ribbon.

n⁰ˢ *15 & 16*

stars and moon t-shirts

photos pages 24–25 • chart page 131

1 t-shirt • DMC 14-count soluble waste canvas • size 26 tapestry needle

1 skein DMC Mouliné stranded cotton: 3845 and 3844 for the stars t-shirt

1 skein DMC Mouliné stranded cotton: 3845, S712 and 3348 for the moon t-shirt

stitch used: cross-stitch

Attach a piece of soluble canvas using large basting stitches to the place you will be embroidering. Begin the motif in the centre of the soluble canvas and cross-stitch over 1 thread of canvas with 2 strands of Mouliné cotton. Remove the soluble canvas by placing the t-shirt under water and rubbing carefully.

n° *17*

fit-for-a-queen bib

photo page 26 • chart page 114

25 x 25 cm polkadot cotton • 25 x 25 cm waffle-weave fabric • 25 x 25 cm pinwale corduroy

DMC 14-count soluble waste canvas • 1.6 m bias binding • size 26 tapestry needle

1 skein DMC Mouliné stranded cotton: 3685 and 150 • stitch used: cross-stitch

Cut out the three pieces of fabric following the pattern on page 92. Baste the waste canvas to the polkadot cotton and embroider the motif with 2 strands of Mouliné cotton over 1 strand of canvas. Lay the corduroy out flat, wrong side up, and place the waffle-weave fabric and cotton on top, right side up. Pin the bias binding around the outside of the bib, then around the neck opening, as per the diagram, and stitch, first of all around the outside of the bib and then around the neck opening. Gently soak the waste canvas away under water.

n^{os} *18 & 19*

sheet and pillowcase

photo page 27 • chart page 115

72 x 127 cm 40-count linen for the sheet • 38 x 65 cm cotton print for the pillowcase

70 cm lace edging • 3 pieces batting, each 34 x 26 cm

DMC 14-count soluble waste canvas • size 26 tapestry needle

1 skein DMC Mouliné stranded cotton: 3802, 3803, 154 and 3685

stitch used: cross-stitch

For the sheet, cross-stitch the motif over 2 threads of linen, using 1 strand of Mouliné cotton, 7 cm from the top and 30 cm from the right edge. Next, machine-sew a 2-cm double hem on each side, then a double hem (turning in 1 cm, then 3 cm) along the bottom, and a double hem (1 then 2 cm) along the top. Sew on the lace by hand along the top edge.

For the pillowcase, baste a piece of soluble canvas to the cotton fabric, so that the motif will be on the front of the pillowcase. Cross-stitch the motif over 1 thread of canvas, using 2 strands of Mouliné cotton. Remove the soluble canvas by placing the fabric in water and rubbing carefully.

Next, stitch a double hem (1 cm, then 2 cm) along the bottom, and press a flap (pressing under 2 cm, then 4 cm) along the top. Fold the fabric as shown on the diagram and stitch the sides, 1 cm from the edge. Turn right side out, press, and insert the three layers of batting inside.

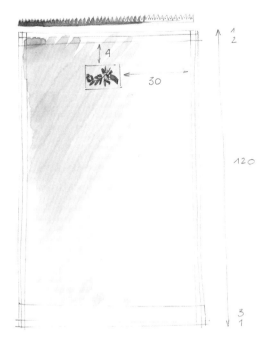

n° 20

this-way-and-that-way quilt cover
photos pages 28–29 • chart pages 116–117
2 pieces white 40-count linen, each 90 x 119 cm
10 x 20-cm lengths white silk ribbon • size 28 tapestry needle
1 skein DMC Mouliné stranded cotton: 640 and 642
stitches used: cross-stitch, satin stitch and stem stitch

Cross-stitch the motifs over 2 linen threads on one rectangle of linen, using 1 strand of Mouliné cotton, positioning them as per the placement diagram. Follow the colour guide on page 117 to embroider the mouse, then sketch in and work the squiggly line in stem stitch. Next, machine-zigzag around each piece of fabric.

Place the two pieces of linen right sides together, then stitch the sides and the top, 1 cm from the edge. Press under 2 cm, then 5 cm for the hem along the bottom edge. Turn the quilt cover right side out, then insert one end of each ribbon into the hem along the bottom, spacing them evenly and making sure they are matched up with each other on each side of the quilt cover. Stitch the hem, being sure to sew in the ribbons.

n° 21

striped jumpsuit
photo page 30 • chart page 118
1 striped jumpsuit
DMC 14-count soluble waste canvas • size 26 tapestry needle
1 skein DMC Mouliné stranded cotton: 3809
stitch used: cross-stitch

Attach a 15 x 25 cm piece of soluble canvas to the middle of the jumpsuit using large basting stitches.
(If your soluble canvas is smaller, you can sew on two pieces, the edge of one aligned under the other).
Begin the motif in the centre of the canvas and cross-stitch over 1 canvas thread with 1 strand of Mouliné
cotton. Remove the soluble canvas by placing the jumpsuit in water and rubbing carefully.

Since it can be difficult to embroider on a soft fabric like jersey, even with waste canvas, you could also
embroider the motif on a piece of linen and then sew it onto the jumpsuit.

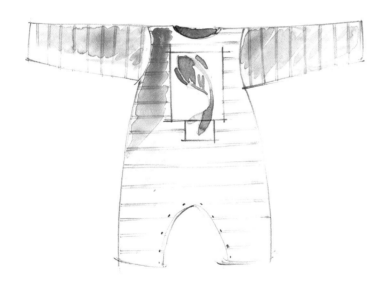

n° 22

little horror bib

photo page 31 • chart page 119

30 x 45 cm 40-count linen • 30 x 45 cm waffle-weave fabric

30 x 45 cm cotton print • 30 x 30 cm cotton with a contrast print

DMC 14-count soluble waste canvas • 2.5 m bias binding • size 28 tapestry needle

1 skein DMC Mouliné stranded cotton: S471, 3765, 3845, 3808 and 3844

stitch used: cross-stitch

Cut out the three rectangles of fabric following the pattern on page 110. Cross-stitch the face motif over 2 threads on the linen, using 1 strand of Mouliné cotton. Press the pocket square in half and round the bottom corners to match the bib pieces. Open out again, baste the waste canvas below the centre fold and cross-stitch the lettering over 1 thread of canvas with 2 strands of cotton.

Remove the soluble canvas gently under water, then dry and press in half again. Baste the pocket on the right side of the linen bib, matching lower edges. Lay the cotton print out flat, wrong side up, and place the waffle-weave fabric and linen on top, right side up. Pin the bias binding around the outside of the bib, then around the neck opening, as per the diagram, and stitch, first around the outside of the bib and ten around the neck opening.

n° 23

my-ball-gown dress cover

photo page 32 • chart pages 120–121

40-count white linen (size depends on the coat hanger: allow an extra 3–4 cm on each side for the hems and 5–6 cm extra length for the hem at the bottom)

1 wooden coat hanger (if it is unfinished wood, it will look nicer if painted white)

2 x 50-cm lengths pink silk ribbon • 50 small glue-on craft jewels • fabric glue

1 skein DMC Mouliné stranded cotton: 605, 600 and 150 • size 28 tapestry needle

stitch used: cross-stitch

Fold the piece of linen in half, right sides together, with the fold at the top. Lay the hanger on the fabric, a few centimetres from the top and trace the curve onto the fabric, 2 cm above the hanger, then cut so that you have two pieces.

Cross-stitch the motif over 2 threads on the piece of linen for the front, using 1 strand of Mouliné cotton. Place the two pieces of fabric right sides together and stitch the curved edge, 2 cm from the edge, leaving a 3–4 cm opening in the centre for the hook.

Press under 1 cm, then another 2 cm, on the side edges. Cut both pieces of ribbon in half and insert them into the hem on each side at the lengthways mid-point. Stitch the hems, catching the ribbon ends in place.

Press and stitch a double hem on the bottom edges, turning up first 2 cm, then 5 cm. Turn the cover right side out and press. Glue the craft jewels to the front with the help of a pair of tweezers, placing the pumpkin design under the linen to trace, if you like. Tie the side ribbons together.

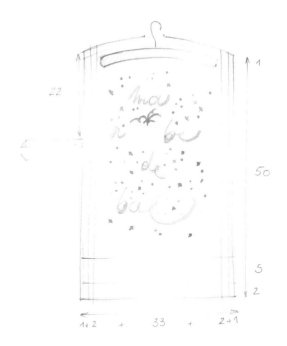

n° 24

counting geese dress
photo page 33 • chart page 122
1 linen dress • size 28 tapestry needle
1 skein DMC Mouliné stranded cotton: 600, 604 and 150
stitch used: cross-stitch

Cross-stitch the motifs on the dress over 2 linen threads using 1 strand of Mouliné cotton, as shown on the placement diagrams, but adjusting the spacing of the motifs along the bottom according to the measurements of the dress. If your linen is not even-weave or the dress is made from a different fabric, you can also baste waste canvas in place for the cross-stitch. You could also cross-stitch the border separately and add it to the dress.

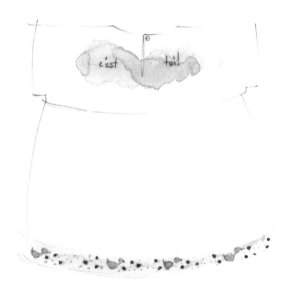

n° 25

a-star-is-born cushion
photo pages 34–35 • chart page 123
45 x 92 cm 40-count linen • 80 cm striped ribbon
1 skein DMC Mouliné stranded cotton: 927, E168 and 928 • size 28 tapestry needle
stitch used: cross-stitch

Cross-stitch the motifs over 2 threads with 1 strand of Mouliné cotton on the piece of linen, using the placement diagram below: the moon at the top right, close to the raw edge, the words at the bottom left, upside-down. Next, press a double hem along the shorter side near where the words are embroidered, turning in 1 cm, then 2 cm. Cut the ribbon in half, tuck the end of one piece under the hem and stitch the hem. Fold the linen in three as shown, right sides together, and stitch the sides, 1 cm from the edge. Turn right side out and press. Sew the end of the other piece of ribbon in place to match the first piece and tie in a bow.

Variation: You can embroider the whole motif or just pick out a detail, for example the moon.

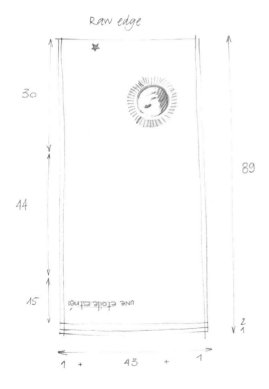

n° 26

quilt

photo pages 36–37 • chart page 126
2 pieces striped cotton, each 71 × 106 cm
3 pieces thin cotton batting, each 70 × 100 cm • size 26 tapestry needle
DMC 14-count soluble waste canvas
1 skein DMC Mouliné stranded cotton: 471, 520, 469, 150, S602, 644, 3781, 472 and 3371
stitches used: cross-stitch and straight stitch

Baste some waste canvas to one of the cotton rectangles, using the placement diagram below as a guide. Cross-stitch the motifs you have chosen over 1 thread of canvas with 2 strands of Mouliné cotton, beginning in the middle of the motif. Work the outlines in straight stitch with 1 strand of cotton. Next, remove the soluble canvas by placing the fabric in water and rubbing carefully.

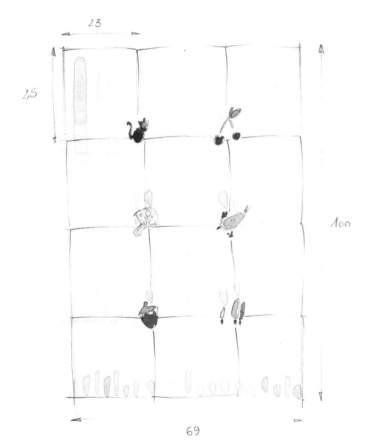

Place the two pieces of fabric right sides together, and stitch the top and sides, 1 cm from the edge. Turn the case right side out and press. Press under a 1 cm hem on the bottom edge, then another 4 cm, and stitch in place.

Insert the batting layers inside, then stitch the opening closed (you can also sew ribbons into the hem then tie them together, like the quilt cover on page 72). To finish, embroider an extra cross in the middle of each motif to quilt the layers.

n° 27

Eiffel Tower alphabet
photo page 38 • chart pages 124–125
50 x 70 cm lavender blue 28-count linen • size 26 tapestry needle
1 skein DMC Mouliné stranded cotton: 3809, 3844, 3765, S471 and 3810
stitch used: cross-stitch

Begin the motif in the centre of the linen and cross-stitch over 2 threads with 2 strands of Mouliné cotton. The embroidered motif only measures about 18 x 32 cm so there will be a large margin around your alphabet, which will particularly set off the design.

n° 28

health record booklet cover
photo page 39 • chart page 127
34 x 26 cm cotton print (outside) • 34 x 26 cm contrast cotton print (inside)
2 pieces contrast cotton print, each 20 x 26 cm (flaps)
34 x 26 cm thin batting • DMC 14-count soluble waste canvas • 1.7 m bias binding
1 skein DMC Mouliné stranded cotton: 3808, 3844 and 3848 • size 26 tapestry needle
stitch used: cross-stitch

Baste a piece of soluble canvas to one half of the fabric for the front cover and, starting in the centre, cross-stitch the motif over 1 strand of canvas using 2 strands of Mouliné cotton. Next, remove the soluble canvas by placing the fabric in water and rubbing carefully.

Lay the cotton for the outside out flat, wrong side up, then place the batting and the cotton for the inside on top, right side up. Fold the flap pieces in half lengthways and place them on top of the three layers of fabric, folded edge towards the centre, as per the diagram. Pin some bias binding all around the sides and stitch, taking an extra piece of bias binding into the seams on the right- and left-hand sides to tie the cover closed.

n° 29

bathrobe

photo page 40 • chart page 140

1 plain white bathrobe • DMC 14-count soluble waste canvas • size 26 tapestry needle

1 skein DMC Mouliné stranded cotton: 645, 642, 3740, 520, 470 and 472

stitch used: cross-stitch

Attach a piece of soluble canvas to the hood using large basting stitches. Begin the motif in the centre of the soluble canvas and cross-stitch over 1 canvas thread with 2 strands of Mouliné cotton. Remove the soluble canvas by placing the hood in water and rubbing carefully.

n° 30

t-shirt

photo page 41 • chart page 130

1 t-shirt • DMC 14-count soluble waste canvas • size 26 tapestry needle

1 skein DMC Mouliné stranded cotton: 3740, 520, 472 and 470

stitch used: cross-stitch

Using large basting stitches, attach a piece of soluble canvas to the place you will be embroidering. Start the motif in the centre of the canvas and cross-stitch over 1 thread with 2 strands of Mouliné cotton. Remove the soluble canvas by placing the t-shirt in water and rubbing carefully.

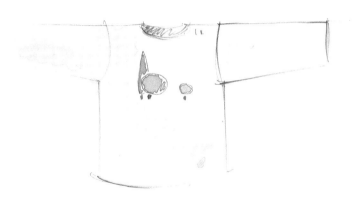

n° 31

Lucie embroidery

photos pages 42–43 • chart pages 128–129 and 134

50 x 30 cm dyed, antique 40-count linen • size 28 tapestry needle

1 skein DMC Mouliné stranded cotton: 600, 815, 603 and E168

stitch used: cross-stitch

Begin the motif in the centre of the piece of fabric and cross-stitch over 2 threads with 1 strand of Mouliné cotton. Personalise your embroidery using the letters and numbers on page 134.

Variation: You can frame this embroidery to hang it on the wall or else embroider it on a piece of linen that's a little larger and make it into a cushion (see the assembly instructions for the bird-on-a-wire cushion page 64).

n° 32

bouquet embroidery

photo page 44 • chart pages 136–139

40 x 30 cm natural 40-count linen

1 skein DMC Mouliné stranded cotton: 822 • size 28 tapestry needle

stitch used: cross-stitch

Begin the motif in the centre of the piece of fabric and cross-stitch over 2 threads with 1 strand of Mouliné cotton. Make sure you leave a margin of at least 10 cm all around so you can frame this embroidery or stretch it over a wooden frame in the same way you stretch a canvas.

n° 33

little girl case
photo page 45 • chart pages 132–133
27 x 42 cm natural 28-count linen
2 pieces cotton print, each 27 x 22 cm
1 button • 1 leather lace • size 26 tapestry needle
1 skein DMC Mouliné stranded cotton: 415, 160 and 317
stitch used: cross-stitch

Centre the motif at the top of the linen rectangle and cross-stitch over 1 thread of linen with 1 strand of Mouliné cotton. Next, fold the linen in half, right sides together, and stitch the sides 1 cm from the edge. Place the two rectangles of cotton right sides together and stitch the sides, 1 cm from the edge. Turn the linen bag right side out and place it inside the cotton casing (the right sides of the two fabrics are thus together), matching the top edges of the two fabrics.

Insert the leather tie between the two layers of fabric, as per the diagram p. 84, then stitch all around the top, 1 cm from the edge, taking the tie into the seam. Next, turn the lining right side out, turn in 1 cm on each side of the opening edges and slipstitch closed. Push the lining back inside the case and sew on a button to correspond with the leather tie.

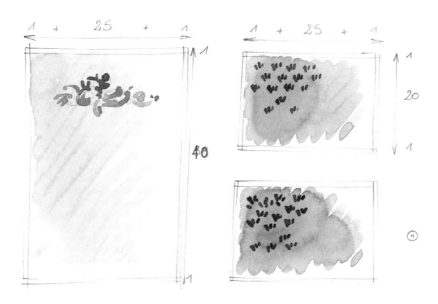

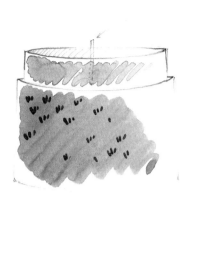

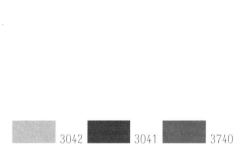

3042	3041	3740

n° 34

little guy embroidery
photo page 49 • chart pages 132–133
50 x 50 cm white 40-count linen
1 skein DMC Mouliné stranded cotton 451, 160 and 317
stitch used: cross-stitch

Begin the motif in the centre of the piece of fabric and cross-stitch over 2 threads with 1 strand of Mouliné cotton. Make sure you leave a margin of at least 10 cm all around so you can frame the embroidery or stretch it over a wooden frame in the same way you stretch a canvas.

n° 35

counting sheep curtain

photos pages 50–51 • charts page 135

1 vintage bolster case, with openwork borders if possible

2 bamboo rods (natural or painted) the width of the window shutters

DMC 14-count soluble waste canvas • size 26 tapestry needle

1 skein DMC Mouliné stranded cotton: 642, 938, 161, 160, 930, 3363, 471 and 3348

stitches used: cross-stitch, straight stitch and backstitch

Unpick the case to obtain a large rectangle of fabric then cut in half (the openwork borders will become the bottom of each curtain). Attach the pieces of soluble canvas to where you will be embroidering using large basting stitches. Position the motifs wherever you like: symmetrically, randomly, in a line… playing "leap-sheep". You can also make room to embroider a date of birth. Cross-stitch over 1 thread with 2 strands of Mouliné cotton, beginning the motifs in the centre of the canvas.

Work the backstitch outlines with 1 strand of cotton, then remove soluble canvas by placing the curtains in water and rubbing carefully. If needed, trim the curtains to adapt them to the size of your window, then make a 2 cm hem each side and a wide casing along the top to hold the bamboo rods. To finish, screw small hooks for the bamboo rods to the window architraves.

Variation: you can embroider everything in cross-stitch but you could also have fun with a few straight stitches for the trunks and use satin stitch for the leaves of the trees. You can also combine the two techniques for the sheep by embroidering the bodies in cross-stitch and the heads in satin stitch.

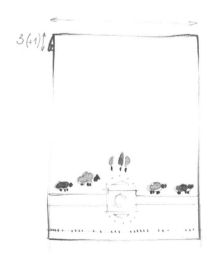

n° 36

butterfly jumpsuit
photo page 52 • chart page 95
1 jumpsuit
DMC 14-count soluble waste canvas • size 26 tapestry needle
1 skein DMC Mouliné stranded cotton: 947, 498 and 605
stitch used: cross-stitch

Attach a piece of soluble canvas using large basting stitches to the place you will be embroidering. Begin the motif in the centre of the soluble canvas and cross-stitch over 1 thread with 2 strands of Mouliné cotton. Once you have embroidered the butterflies, remove the soluble canvas by placing the jumpsuit in water and and rubbing carefully.

n° 37

just-a-minute bottle cover

photo page 53 • chart page 140

30 x 32 cm white 40-count linen

1 x 9-cm diameter circle white 40-count linen • 30 cm ribbon

1 skein DMC Mouliné stranded cotton: 931, 932 and 160 • size 28 tapestry needle

stitch used: cross-stitch

Cross-stitch the motif over 2 threads using 1 strand of Mouliné cotton in the middle of the linen rectangle. Next fold the linen in half as per the diagram below, right sides together, and stitch the sides together, 1 cm from the edge, to form a tube. Sew on the base, stitching 1 cm from the edge.

Turn down a double hem (1 cm, then 3 cm) around the top edge, and stitch to form a drawstring casing, leaving an opening for the ribbon. Turn right side out and thread the ribbon through the casing with the help of a safety pin.

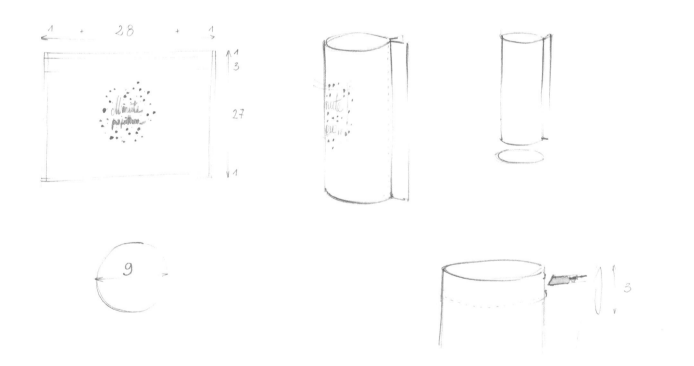

n° 38

cot bumper

photo page 54 • chart page 141

140 x 69 cm vintage sheet with a monogram • 140 x 140 cm batting
140 x 70 cm cotton for the lining • DMC 14-count soluble waste canvas
4 x 30 cm lengths white mousseline ribbon • 4 x 30 cm lengths striped ribbon
1 skein DMC Mouliné stranded cotton: 799, 159, S932, S931 and S712 • size 26 tapestry needle
stitches used: cross-stitch and straight stitch

Using large basting stitches, attach pieces of soluble canvas to where the embroideries will be placed, then cross-stitch over 1 thread with 2 strands of Mouliné cotton, beginning the motifs at the centre of the canvas. Once you have finished embroidering the motifs, remove the soluble canvas by placing the fabric in water and rubbing carefully.

Lay the batting out flat, place the cotton on top, right side up, then the linen, wrong side up. Insert the striped and white pieces of ribbon in pairs along the top (14 groups of 2 ribbons), spacing them regularly, so they are sewn into the seam. Stitch the sides and the top, 1 cm from the edge, and turn right side out, bringing the linen over the top of the batting. Turn in 1 cm on each of the bottom opening edges and stitch (trimming the batting a little if you need to).

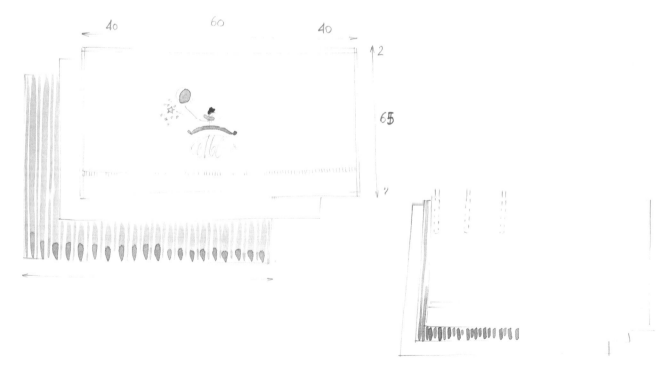

n° 39

alphabet sampler

photo page 55 • chart pages 142–143

60 x 40 cm pale blue 40-count linen • size 28 tapestry needle

1 skein DMC Mouliné stranded cotton: 160, S471, 762, S712 and E677

stitch used: cross-stitch

Begin the motif in the centre of the fabric and cross-stitch over 2 threads with 1 or 2 strands of Mouliné cotton.

Variation: You can frame this embroidery for hanging or else embroider it on a piece of linen that's a bit larger and make it into a cushion (see the instructions for assembling the bird-on-a-wire cushion page 64).

Enlarge to 140%

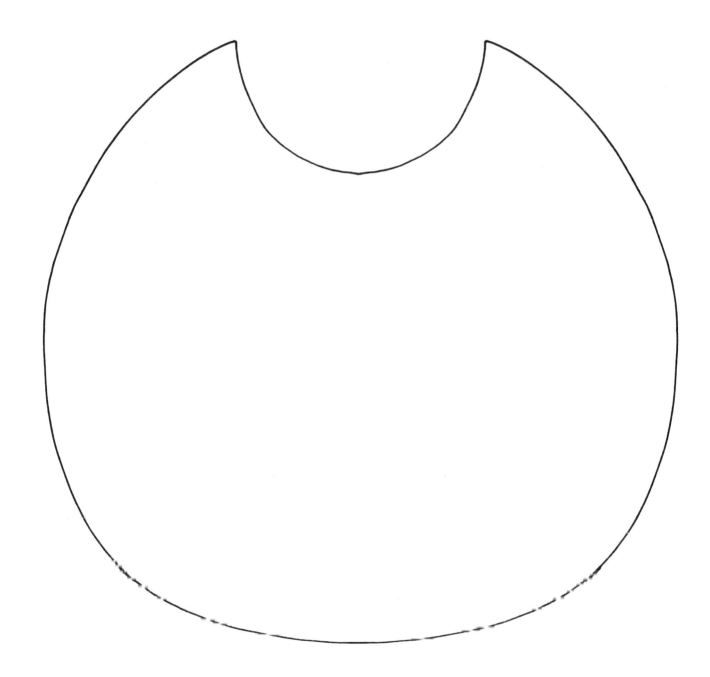

Enlarge to 135%

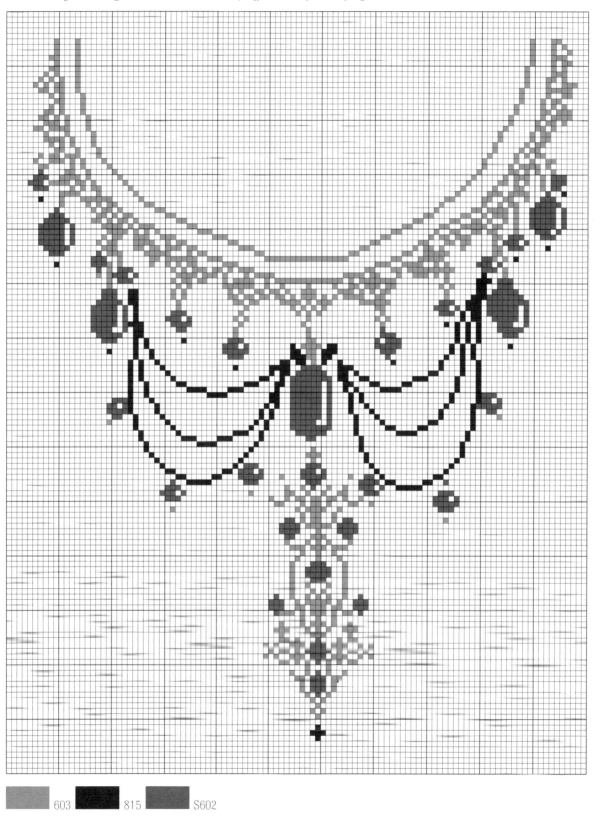

603   815   S602

963   947   498   605

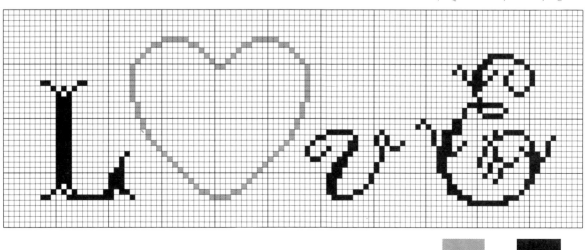

S712   415

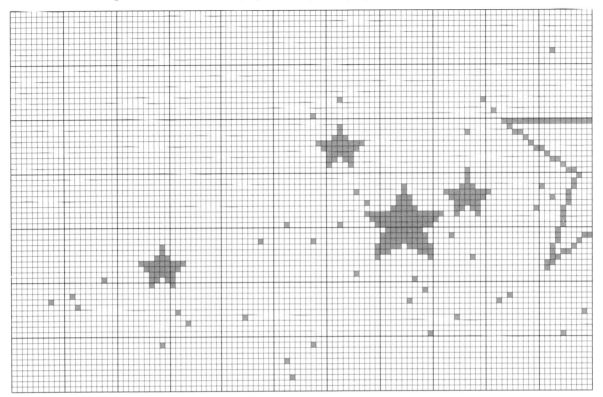

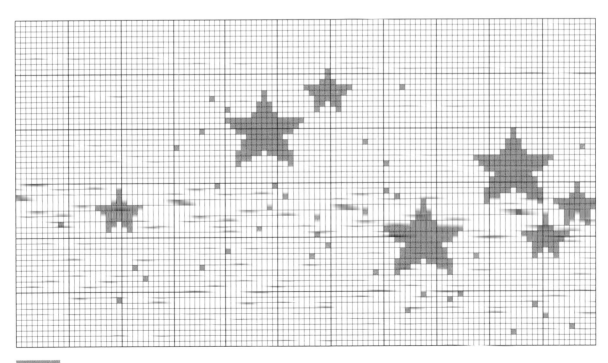

E168

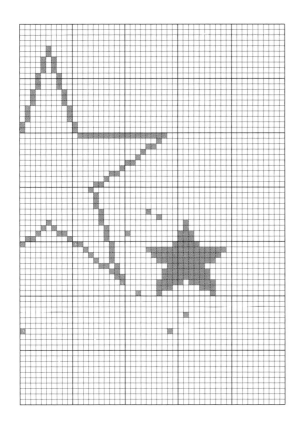

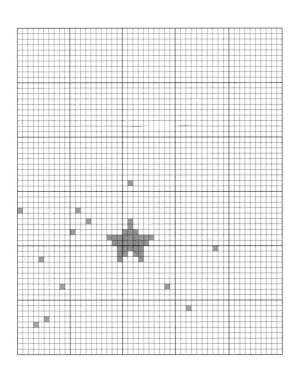

451

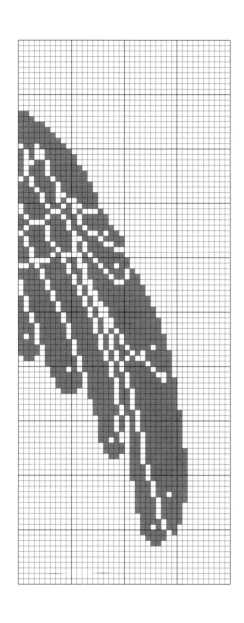

If you would like to make these wings but are short on time, just embroider the outlines using this diagram as a guide.

154 600

600　150　777

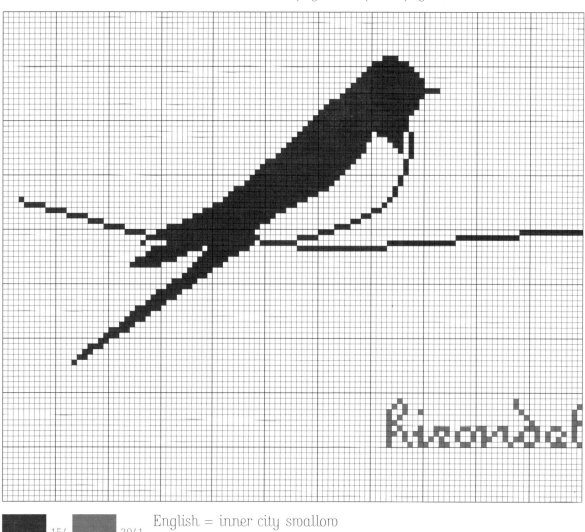

154   3041   English = inner city swallow

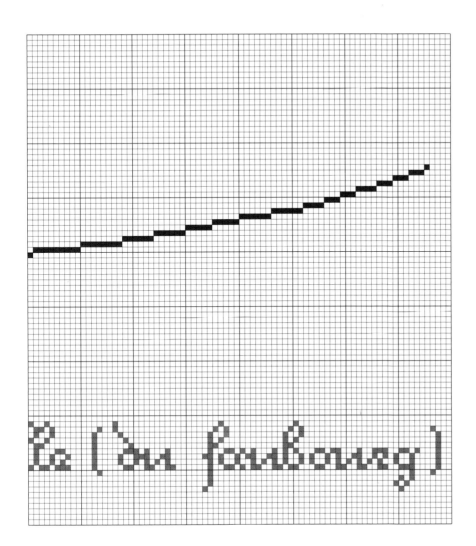

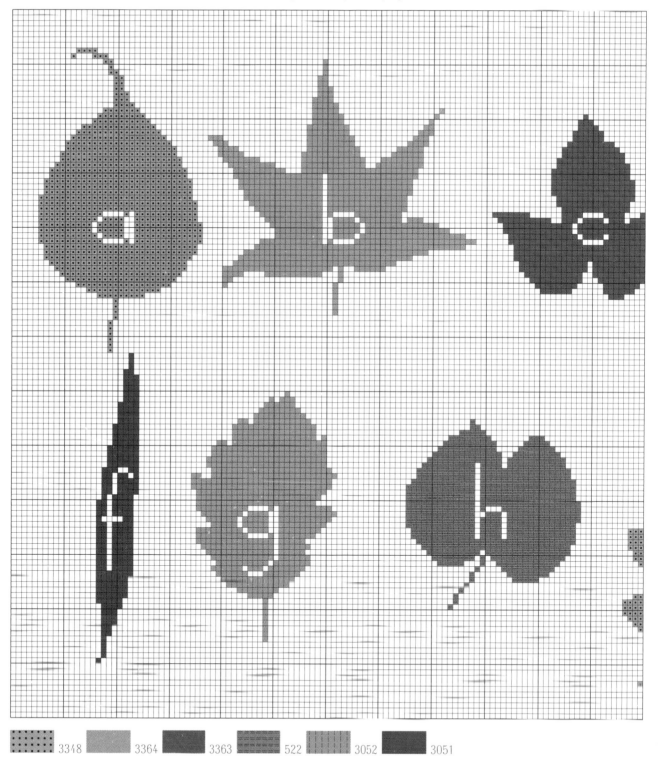

3348   3364   3363   522   3052   3051

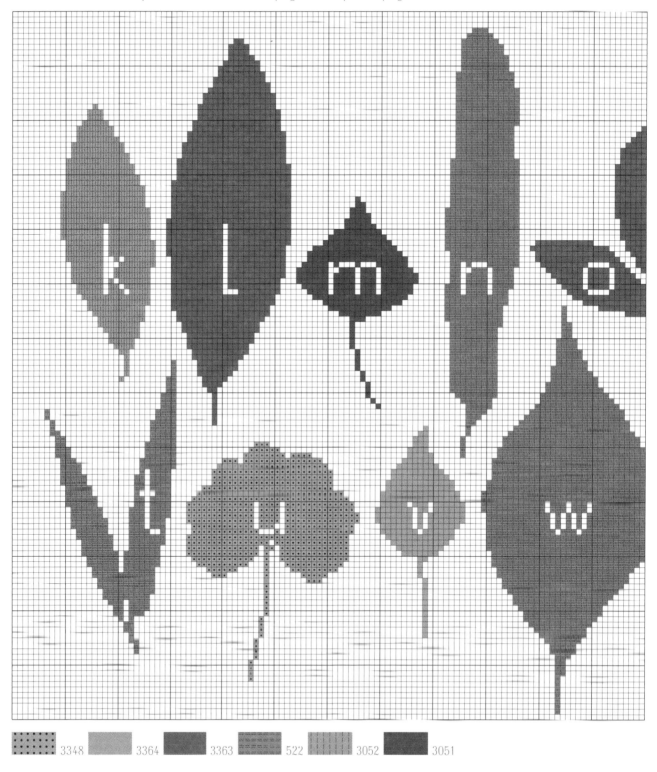

| | 3348 | | 3364 | | 3363 | | 522 | | 3052 | | 3051 |

E168 3760 3844 471 154 English = 'travel keeps you young'

3809 500 522 947

Pocket

Enlarge to 150%

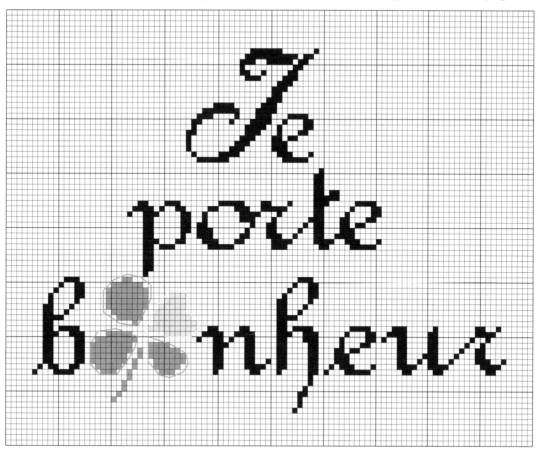

English = I bring good luck

154   S472   S471

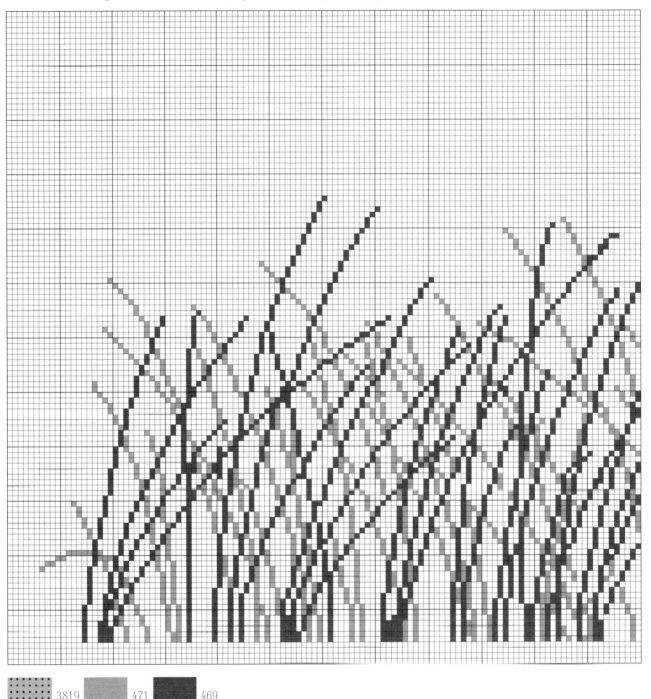

3819 471 469

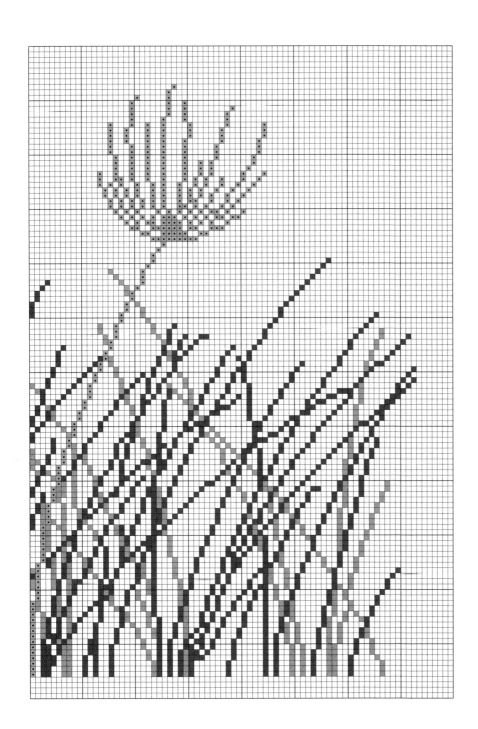

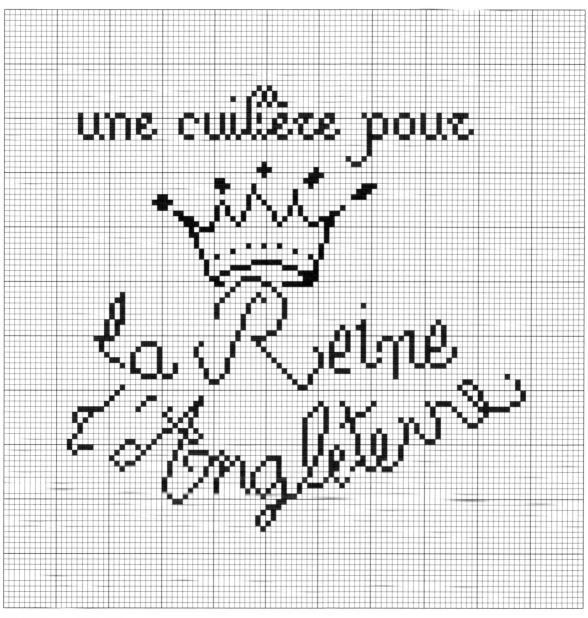

▓ 3685	▓ 150	English – a spoonful for the Queen of England

n°ˢ 18 & 19
sheet and pillowcase
instructions page *71* • photo page *27*

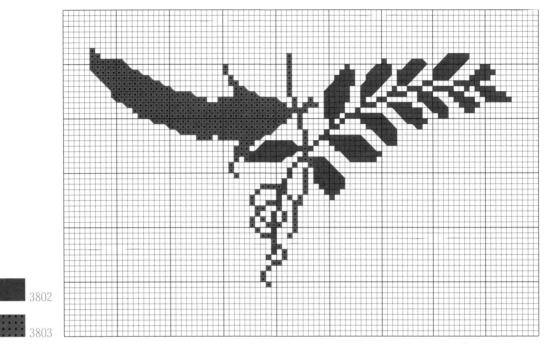

3802

3803

154   3685

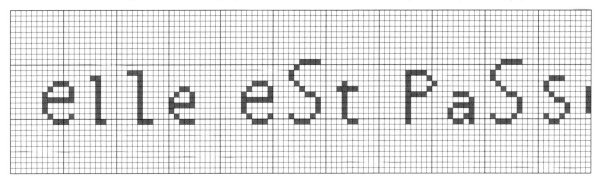

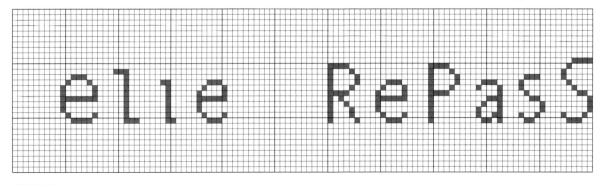

English = she went this way … she'll come back that way

642

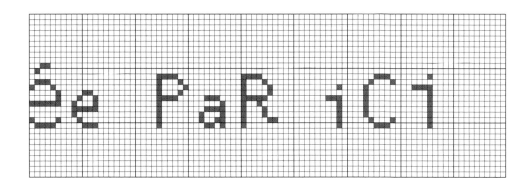

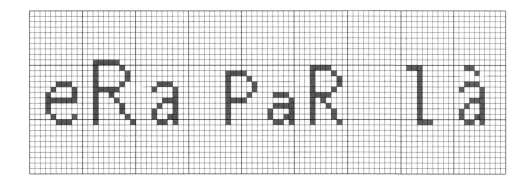

Actual size.
Adjust the size of your mouse to the size of your fabric.

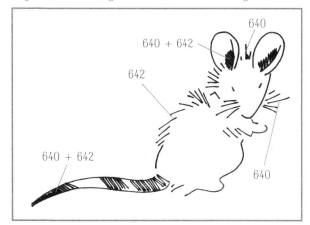

642 640

3809

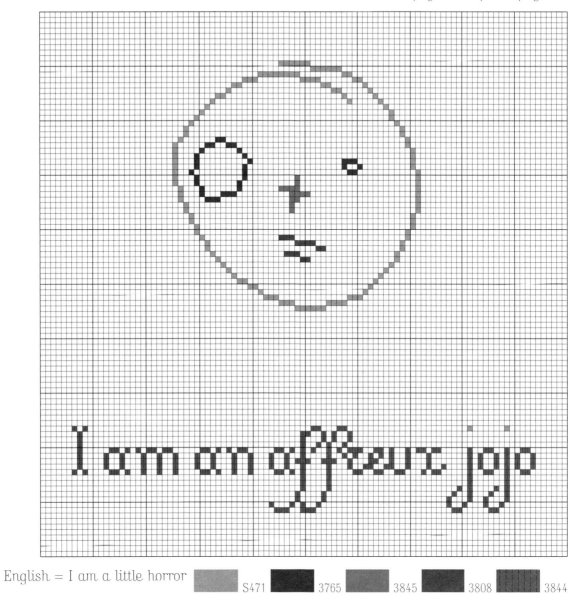

English = I am a little horror

S471 3765 3845 3808 3844

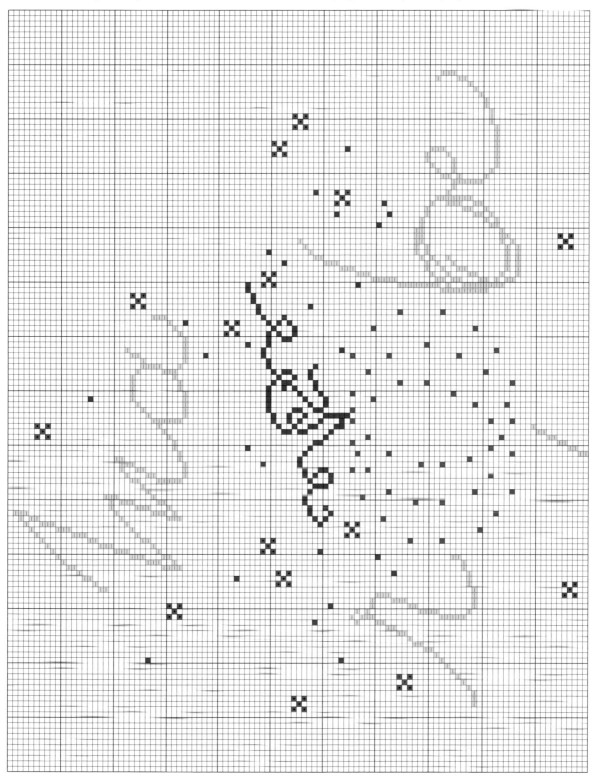

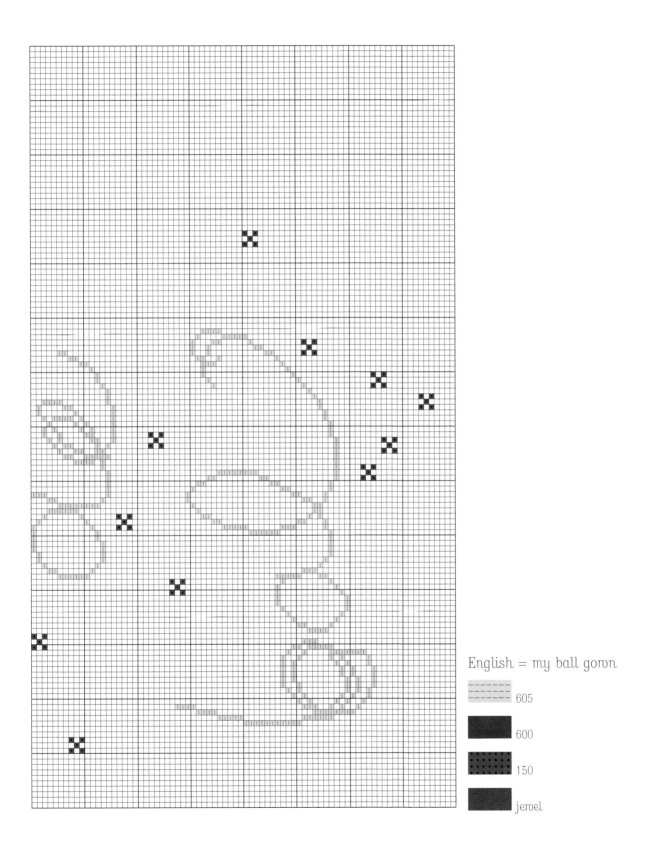

English = my ball goron

605

600

150

jewel

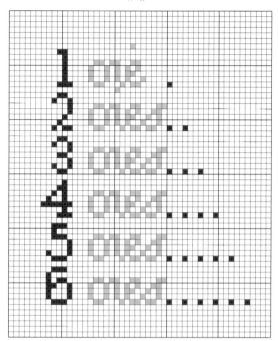

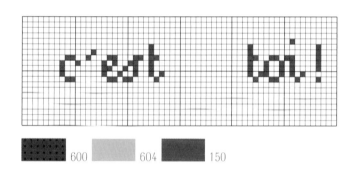

600   604   150

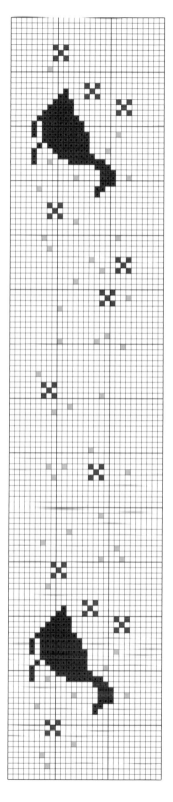

926

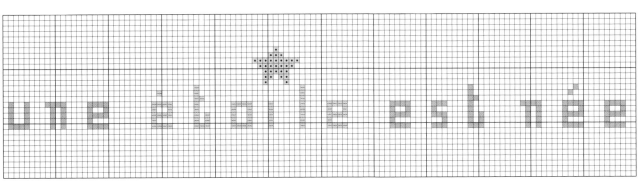

English = a star is born   927   E168   928

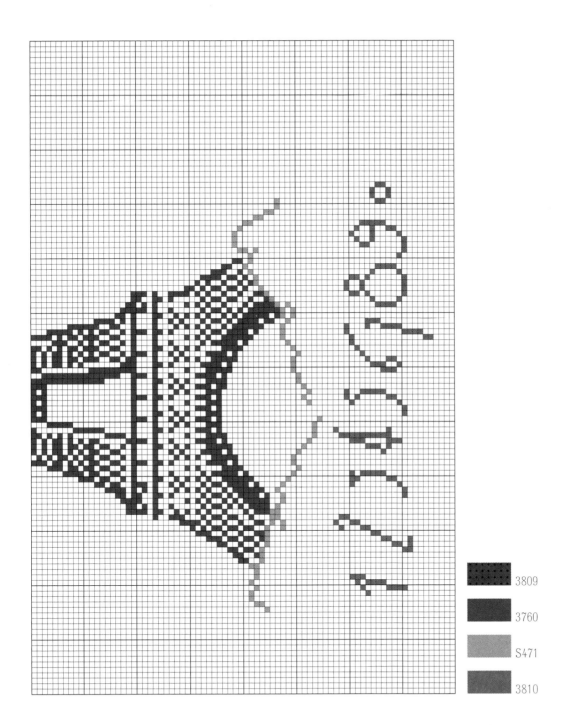

▨	3809
■	3760
▨	S471
▨	3810

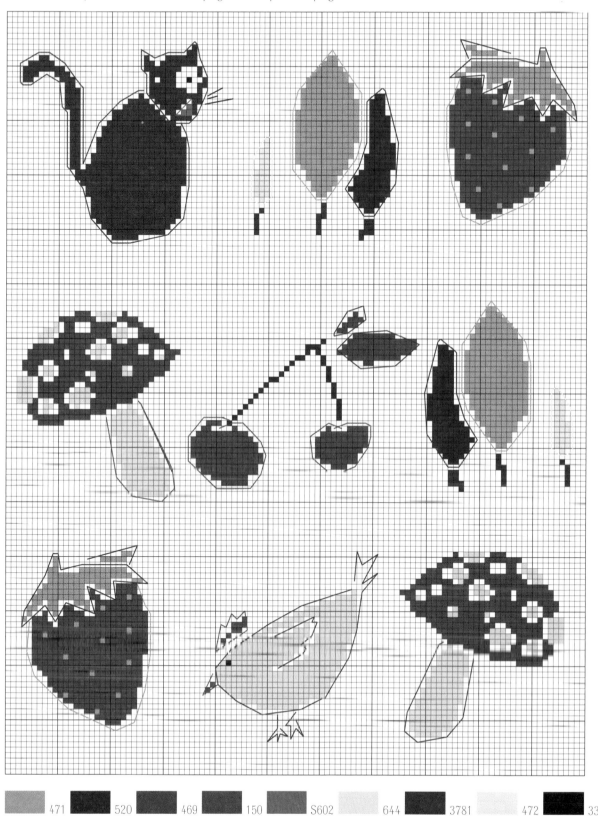

	471		520		469		150		S602		644		3781		472		3371

3808   3844   3848

815   600   603   E168

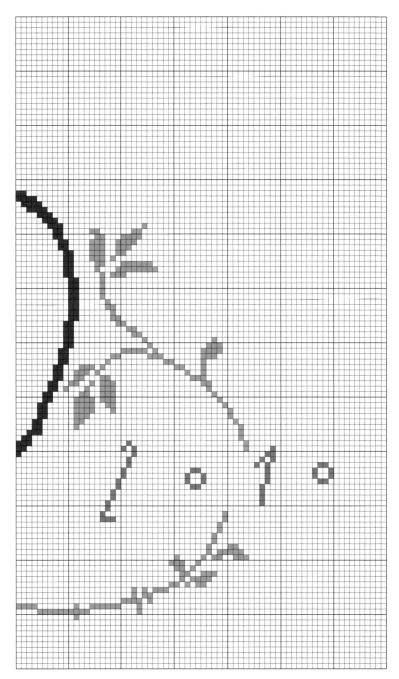

Letters & numbers p. 134.

n^{os} *5 & 6* strawberry and heart t-shirts • instructions page *61* • photos pages *10-11*

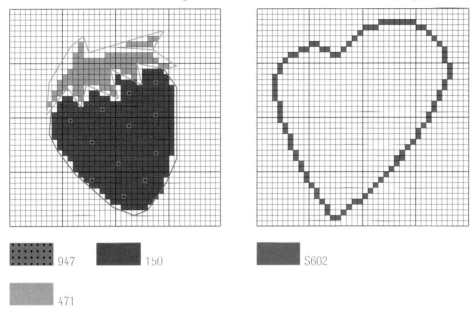

947	150	S602
471		

$n°$ *30* t-shirt • instructions page *81* • photo page *41*

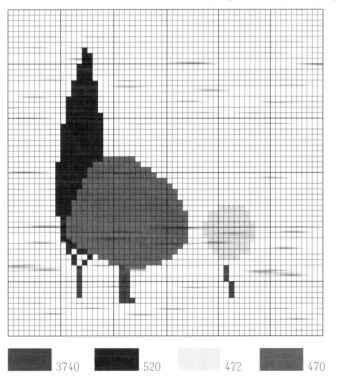

3740	520	472	470

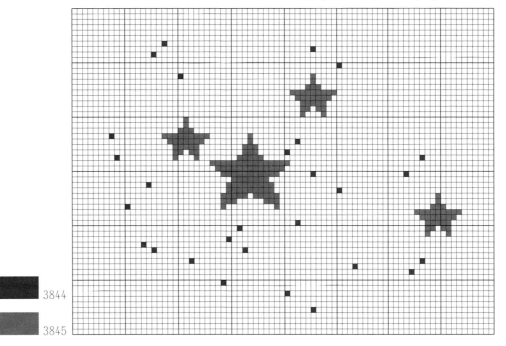

▇	3844
▇	3845

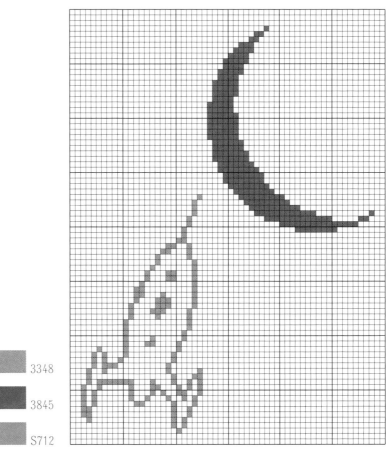

▇	3348
▇	3845
▇	S712

415   160   317

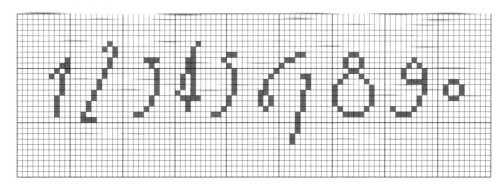

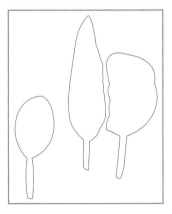

Actual size.
Adapt the size of the trees
to the size of your fabric.

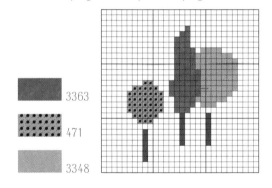

3363

471

3348

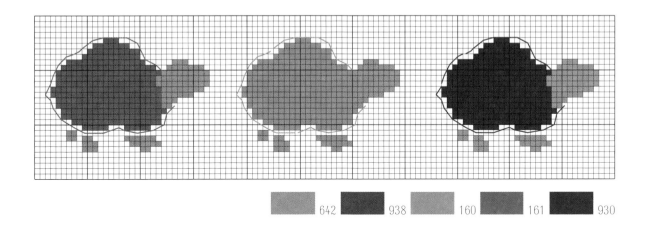

642 938 160 161 930

1

822

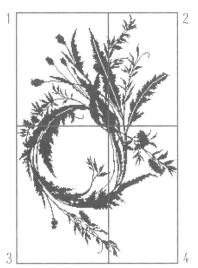

2

Placement diagram.

n° 29 bathrobe • instructions page **81** • photo page **40**

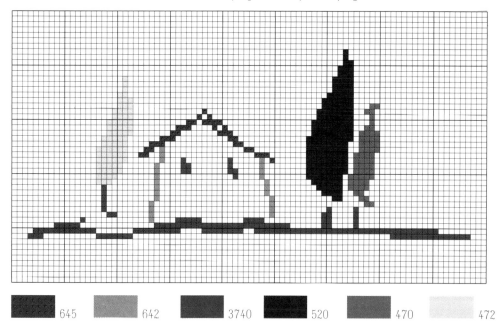

645   642   3740   520   470   472

n° 37 just-a-minute bottle cover • instructions page **87** • photo page **53**

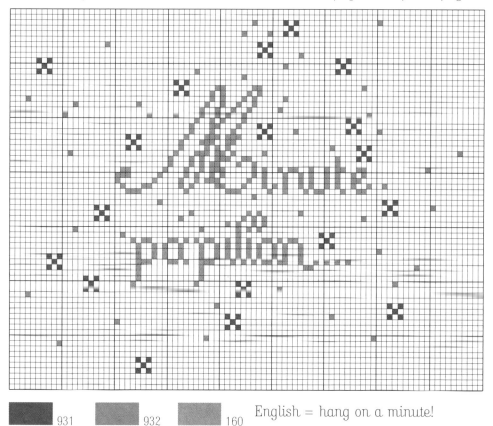

931   932   160   English = hang on a minute!

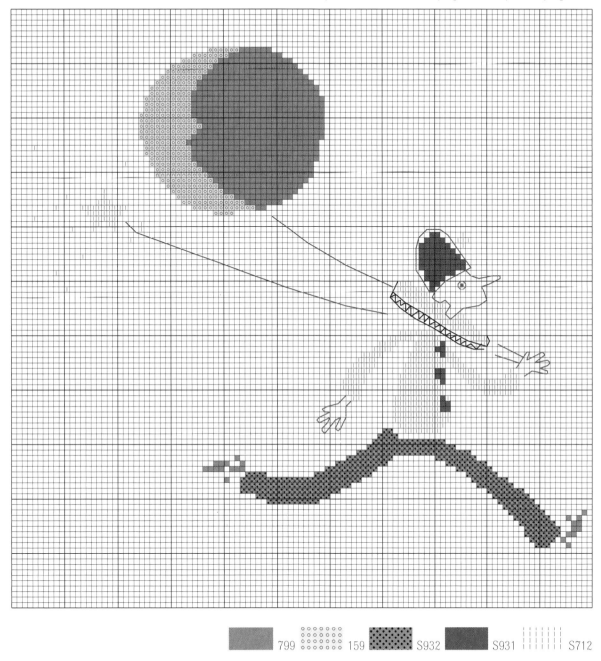

799	159	S932	S931	S712

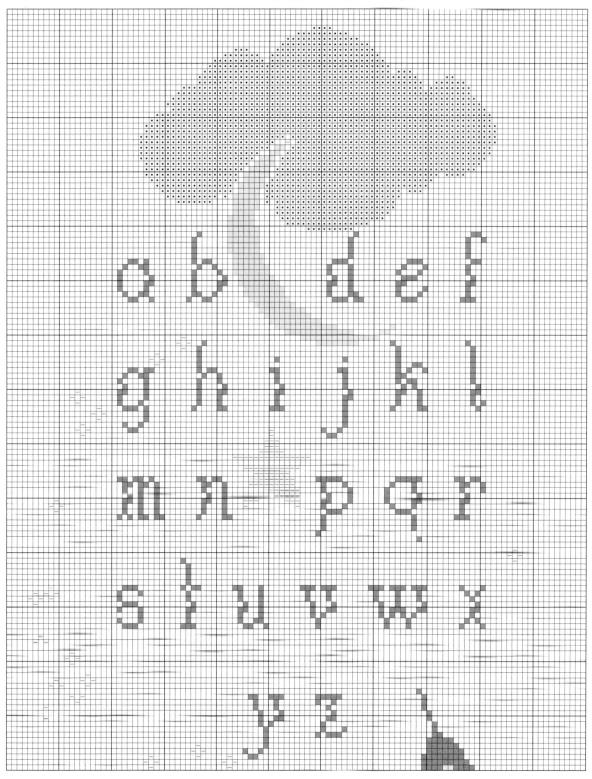

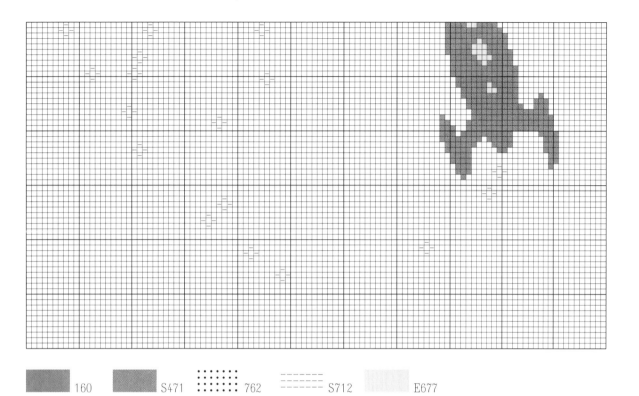

160 S471 762 S712 E677

Acknowledgements

Endless thanks to my Fairy Godmothers at Entrée des fournisseurs for their wonderful linens, shimmering ribbons, incredible buttons, but above all for the laughs, advice and biscuits… May they know once and for all how precious they are to me.

A curtsey to Corinne Valette and all the team at DMC for their trust right from the beginning, their kindness and… the sublime colours of their threads! Thank you.

Kisses to Anne, Corinne and all the team at La Droguerie, where I have hung out with my mother and my grandmother since it opened (I was 5 years old!). The entrance to the shop, the wool, the delicious jars, the damn (and I'm being polite…) step in the middle of the store always have the same effect on me and that's a comfort in this world of barbarians. Thank you.

Thanks and more to my grandmother for her invaluable help with sewing, without her I would still be there! Thank you, thank you, thank you. Thanks to Maman for having passed all of that down to me and even more! Thanks to Papa for the ti'punch drinks and little snacks that lift the spirits. I love you.

An enormous thank-you to Pascale for the Friday coffees, for her faith and her enthusiasm; I am very touched by this beautiful friendship. Long may it last! All my admiration to Hiroko and Vania for their magnificent work, thanks to both of you… and to Denis for his help! The patience of Dominique, who was lumbered with the instructions, leaves me speechless… I would not have liked to be in her place! Thank you Dominique. Finally, lots of kisses to little Mona, Zélie and Mia… their little faces light up this book.

May the brilliant inventors of 100 Idées be forever blessed, may they know that the women of my family, regardless of generation, are devoted readers still today (we have at least 2 complete sets!). I am tempted to have their logo tatooed on my shoulder!

This book is dedicated to sweet Nathalie, creator of LILI POINTS, with whom I talked about this project so much and who left us before we had a chance to flick through these pages together over a cup of tea. May she find thread in heaven! A thought for Caroline.

First published by Marabout (Hachette Livre) in 2010.
This edition published in 2011 by Murdoch Books Pty Limited

Murdoch Books Australia
Pier 8/9
23 Hickson Road
Millers Point NSW 2000
Phone: +61 (0) 2 8220 2000
Fax: +61 (0) 2 8220 2558
www.murdochbooks.com.au

Murdoch Books UK Limited
Erico House, 6th Floor
93–99 Upper Richmond Road
Putney, London SW15 2TG
Phone: +44 (0) 20 8785 5995
Fax: +44 (0) 20 8785 5985
www.murdochbooks.co.uk

Photography: Hiriko Mori
Stylist: Vania Leroy-Thuillier

Publisher: Diana Hill
Translator: Melissa McMahon
Editor: Georgina Bitcon
Project Editor: Laura Wilson
Production: Joan Beal

Copyright © Marabout (Hachette Livre) 2010
The moral right of the author has been asserted.

National Library of Australia Cataloguing-in-Publication entry
Author: Leloup, Isabelle.
Title: Cross-stitch and embroidery for babies,
               toddlers and children/ Isabelle Leloup.
ISBN: 978-1-74266-130-8 (pbk.)
Series: Made in France.
Notes: Includes index.
Subjects: Cross-stitch, Cross-stitch, Patterns.
Dewey Number: 746.443

A catalogue record for this book is available from the British Library.

Printed by 1010 Printing International Limited, China.

Addresses

Many of these lovely French shops have English sites and mail order.

Entrée des fournisseurs
8 rue des Francs-Bourgeois
75004 Paris
Tel: 01 48 87 58 98
www.entreedesfournisseurs.fr

DMC
www.dmc.fr

La Droguerie
9/11 rue du Jour
75001 Paris
Tel: 01 45 08 93 27
www.ladroguerie.com

Du pareil au même
www.dpam.com

Tissus Grégoire
309 route du 19-Mars-1962
84450 Saint-Saturnin-lès-Avignon
Tel: 04 90 22 21 62
www.tissus-gregoire.fr

Serendipity
81/83 rue du Cherche-Midi
75006 Paris
Tel: 01 40 46 01 15
www.serendipity.fr

Adeline Klam
37 rue Galilée
75016 Paris
Tel: 01 40 70 96 20
www.adelineklam.com